Where Pain Becomes Power

Ivy CB

Where Pain Becomes Power

Ivy CB

Published by Ivy CB, 2024.

WHERE PAIN BECOMES POWER

First edition. November 14, 2024.

ISBN: 979-8227562173

Written by Ivy CB.

Also by Ivy CB

Love in the Metaverse
Love in the Metaverse
Love Beyond the Veil

Standalone
Unshackled: Breaking Free from Fear and Embracing Your
True Self
Where Pain Becomes Power

Table of Contents

Dedication:

To those who have faced hardship and emerged stronger.

May you find the strength to rise, even in your darkest moments.

Epigraph:

"The wound is the place where the Light enters you."

— Rumi

Contents

Dedication

Introduction

We've all heard the saying, "What doesn't kill you makes you stronger." While this may sound like a cliché, there is a deeper truth embedded in these words: our pain has the potential to transform us. The challenges we face are not just obstacles; they are opportunities for growth, resilience, and reinvention. In this book, we will explore how to turn our most difficult experiences into sources of power. Each chapter of Where Pain Becomes Power will focus on a different aspect of this transformative process. From shifting our mindset to embracing vulnerability, from understanding the psychology behind resilience to taking actionable steps toward healing, this book will be your guide to turning adversity into strength. Whether you're dealing with personal loss, overcoming failure, or simply seeking more courage in your day-to-day life, the tools and strategies you'll find here will empower you to face life's challenges with confidence. The goal is not to eliminate pain but to empower you to harness it as a driving force for a more meaningful, empowered life.

Preface

In every life, there comes a time when pain seems overwhelming. It might be a loss, a failure, or the weight of circumstances beyond our control. But what if we could view these painful moments differently? What if they were not just burdens, but opportunities for transformation? Where Pain Becomes Power is a journey of embracing adversity, facing our fears, and using them as fuel to drive us toward our greatest selves. This book isn't about denying the pain we experience; it's about reimagining its role in our lives. Through the following pages, I will guide you through the process of turning hardship into strength—finding power in the very moments we think will break us. You'll discover practical tools, personal stories, and empowering lessons to help you transform your pain into a force that propels you forward. This journey isn't easy, but I believe that the greatest power lies within you, waiting to be unlocked. So, let us begin, together, in the pursuit of strength that emerges from even the darkest times.

Prologue

The first time I truly understood the transformative power of pain, I was standing at the edge of a crossroads. My life had been turned upside down by a sudden loss—one that left me questioning everything I thought I knew about strength. I wasn't sure how to move forward, or if I even could. But as I took the first step into the unknown, I realized something remarkable: I wasn't alone. The pain I felt wasn't just a weight to bear—it was a bridge to something greater. It became a tool that forced me to confront parts of myself I had long ignored. And in that darkness, I began to find the light. What I learned through that journey was simple, yet profound: pain is not our enemy; it is our teacher. This book is my offering to you, the reader, as you embark on your own journey of transformation. If you are facing hardship, or simply want to understand how to turn pain into power, know that you are not alone. You have the strength within you to rise, no matter how heavy the weight feels. Let this be the first step toward discovering that power.

The Promise of Pain

Pain often arrives unannounced. It can come as a jolt, shaking us to our core, or it can seep into our lives slowly, settling in quietly until we finally realize how much it has taken root. No matter how it shows up, pain has a way of changing us, sometimes so deeply that we can hardly recognize who we were before it. But what if, instead of resisting pain, we could find a way to harness it? To use it, even, as a stepping stone toward something greater?

This book is about that journey—the journey where pain becomes power. It doesn't promise a way around pain, because there is no easy way to bypass the hard moments in life. It doesn't promise quick fixes or simple solutions, because learning to embrace pain requires courage, patience, and compassion for ourselves. What it does offer is a path forward, a way to transform pain into something more meaningful.

Over the years, I have come to see that pain—whether physical, emotional, or spiritual—is one of life's greatest teachers. I've watched people rise from unimaginable challenges with a renewed sense of purpose, strength, and compassion. This isn't because they were born with some extraordinary ability to endure hardship. It's because they learned to face pain head-on, to welcome it, even, as a part of their growth. Through their experiences and stories, I came to understand that while pain may leave scars, those scars can serve as reminders of our strength, our resilience, and our capacity for transformation.

You, too, have this capacity. No matter where you are or what you are facing, I invite you to journey with me through the pages of this book. Together, we'll explore how to face pain with courage, how to find strength in vulnerability, and how to rebuild ourselves in ways that make us even stronger. If you're ready, let's begin.

Chapter 1: The Universality of Pain

Pain does not discriminate. It touches every person, every heart, in one way or another. Whether it's the heartache of a lost relationship, the emptiness after a loved one's death, the frustration of personal failure, or the silent battle of mental health struggles—pain finds its way into our lives. It's easy to look around and feel that we're alone in our suffering, that others are somehow shielded from life's hardships. But if we could see beyond the masks we wear, we would see a different reality. We would see that pain is as universal as love, as natural as breath.

In every life, there are moments when everything feels heavy, when the weight of circumstances feels too much to bear. In those moments, we may wonder why we must suffer, why pain must be a part of life. This question has lingered through centuries, pondered by philosophers, writers, and spiritual leaders alike. While we may never fully understand why pain exists, we can learn to approach it in ways that help us grow rather than shrink.

Pain as a Common Thread

Think for a moment about the people in your life—your friends, family, coworkers, even strangers you pass by on the street. Each one of them has experienced pain, and each one is carrying their own story. Maybe it's a mother who's lost a child, a young person navigating the uncertainties of adulthood, or an elderly man who's facing the loss of independence. Pain doesn't look the same for everyone, but it's there, woven into the fabric of our shared humanity.

One of the most powerful ways to cope with pain is to recognize that we are not alone in it. This understanding helps to create a sense of connection, a reminder that suffering is not a sign of failure or weakness. Instead, it's a reflection of our humanity. In sharing our pain, even in small ways, we offer others permission to share theirs as well, and in doing so, we create a community of resilience and understanding.

Different Faces of Pain

Pain wears many faces. For some, it's a silent struggle, carried alone in the privacy of their mind and heart. For others, it's a visible wound that they wear openly. The woman who bravely speaks about her past trauma, the man who mourns the end of a relationship, the child who faces bullying at school—each one experiences pain in a different way. And yet, beneath the surface, the essence of their suffering is the same. It's a longing for relief, for healing, and for the strength to carry on.

Pain is also an equalizer. It doesn't matter how much money you have, where you come from, or what you believe. When life throw challenges your way, all those differences fade into the background. In those moments, we are simply human—vulnerable, seeking comfort, and hoping for peace.

Learning from Others' Journeys

In my own journey, and in the journeys of others I've met, I've come to see that the people who inspire us most are often those who have walked through the fire and come out on the other side. They are the ones who have learned to carry their pain, not as a burden, but as a badge of resilience. These people remind us that pain is not the end of the story. Instead, it can be the beginning of a journey toward a new and stronger self.

Sample Story

Take, for example, the story of Maya, a woman who lost her partner unexpectedly in a car accident. She shared that in the immediate aftermath, her world felt shattered. Grief took hold of her in ways she couldn't control, making even the simplest tasks feel monumental. But as time passed, she found herself learning how to live with her loss. She took up painting, a hobby she had long forgotten, as a way to process her emotions. Slowly, she turned her pain into art, creating pieces that reflected the complexity of her grief and the strength she found in honoring her partner's memory. Today, Maya's artwork speaks to others going through their own losses, reminding them that while the pain may never fully disappear, it can be transformed into something meaningful.

Maya's story reminds us that pain can be a powerful motivator for change and growth. When we allow ourselves to confront it, to sit with it, we may find that it begins to shape us in ways we hadn't anticipated. Instead of hardening us, it can soften us, opening us up to new parts of ourselves that we might never have discovered otherwise.

Finding Connection in Shared Struggles

As we journey together through this book, let us keep in mind that we are walking alongside countless others who have faced their own pain and have found their way to the other side. In each chapter, you will encounter stories like Maya's, reflections on the power of vulnerability, and gentle guidance for embracing your own path of transformation. You are not alone in this journey. Pain may be a part of life, but it doesn't have to define your life. Instead, it can become a source of strength, a reminder of your resilience, and a pathway to a deeper, more compassionate understanding of yourself and others.

Chapter 2: The Initial Shock of Pain

Pain, especially when it arrives suddenly, has a way of shaking us. It can leave us feeling disoriented, vulnerable, and even powerless. When faced with unexpected loss, betrayal, or disappointment, our first instinct is often to shield ourselves, to build walls and create distance between ourselves and the hurt. This initial shock is a natural response, part of how we are wired to protect ourselves from harm. Yet, in understanding this reaction, we can begin to find ways to move forward.

When pain first hits, it's normal to feel a range of emotions that may seem overwhelming. These emotions might not make sense at first. One moment, you might feel numb; the next, you're flooded with anger, sadness, or even guilt. This emotional roller coaster can feel out of control, as though you're caught in a storm without any solid ground. But just as storms eventually pass, the intensity of these feelings will subside too. The key is to understand what's happening inside us, so we can begin to make peace with it.

Our Body's Response to Pain

When we experience pain, our bodies respond instinctively. This response, often called the "fight or flight" reaction, is our body's way of preparing us to face a perceived threat. Whether the pain is physical—like an injury—or emotional—like the end of a relationship—our body reacts with a surge of adrenaline and cortisol, the stress hormones that help us cope with immediate challenges.

In these moments, you might notice your heart pounding, your muscles tensing, or your breath becoming shallow. These physical responses are reminders that our bodies and minds are deeply connected. Emotional pain is not "all in your head"—it's a real, embodied experience that affects us on every level.

Learning to recognize these bodily signals can be the first step in understanding our pain. When we feel the wave of adrenaline or the tightness in our chest, we can remind ourselves that it's a natural response, a sign that our body is working hard to help us cope. It's okay to feel this way. Allowing ourselves to acknowledge the physical impact of pain, rather than pushing it aside, is an important part of healing.

The Emotional Flood

Beyond the physical response, the initial stages of pain often bring a flood of emotions. Shock, denial, anger, sadness—these are just a few of the emotions that may surface. They can feel overwhelming, like a tidal wave that threatens to pull us under. We may even start to judge ourselves for feeling certain emotions, thinking that we shouldn't feel angry or that we should be able to "get over it" quickly.

But emotions are not meant to be ignored or denied. In fact, they are essential parts of our healing process. Emotions help us make sense of what has happened, and they give us clues about what we need in order to heal. The anger we feel, for example, might be a response to a sense of injustice or betrayal, while sadness might reflect the depth of our loss. When we honor these emotions without judgment, we create space for them to be felt and, eventually, to be released.

Sample Story

Consider the story of Aaron, a man who lost his job after dedicating years of hard work and loyalty to his company. For days after hearing the news, he was numb, going through the motions of daily life without really processing what had happened. Then, as the reality set in, anger took hold. He was furious at the unfairness, feeling that his commitment had been tossed aside without a second thought. Next came the sadness—a deep, hollow feeling of grief for the career he had lost, for the relationships he'd built, and for the future he'd envisioned.

At first, Aaron tried to suppress these emotions, telling himself he needed to "stay strong" and move on. But the more he ignored them, the more they seemed to control him, leading to sleepless nights and moments of overwhelming frustration. Finally, he began to allow himself to feel each emotion as it came, letting the anger wash over him, acknowledging the sadness without judgment. Through this process, Aaron found that by accepting his emotions, he was able to begin healing from his loss. He wasn't moving on immediately, but he was learning to move through his pain.

Why Suppression Doesn't Work

It's common to want to suppress painful emotions, especially if we've been taught to view them as weaknesses. But in reality, suppressing emotions only buries them deeper, where they continue to affect us, sometimes in ways we don't even realize. Unacknowledged pain has a way of surfacing in our lives, showing up as anxiety, irritability, or even physical symptoms like headaches and fatigue.

Imagine holding a beach ball underwater. You can keep it submerged for a while, but eventually, it will shoot up to the surface, often with more force than before. Suppressing emotions works in a similar way. The more we try to keep them hidden, the stronger they become when they finally resurface. Allowing ourselves to feel pain openly, even if it's uncomfortable, helps us prevent it from gaining power over us in the long run.

Creating Space for Emotions

One of the most powerful things we can do in the face of pain is to create space for our emotions. This doesn't mean wallowing or letting our emotions take over completely. It simply means giving ourselves permission to feel without rushing to "fix" everything. This might look like setting aside a few minutes each day to check in with ourselves, to ask what we're feeling and why. It might mean journaling our thoughts, talking to a trusted friend, or even sitting in silence, allowing the emotions to rise and fall like waves.

Creating space for emotions also means being kind to ourselves. We can remind ourselves that there's no right or wrong way to feel, and that healing doesn't follow a set timeline. By honoring our emotions, we learn to navigate the initial shock of pain with compassion and understanding.

Sample Exercise: Sitting with the Pain

Here's a simple exercise you can try the next time you're feeling overwhelmed by pain:

1. Find a quiet space where you won't be interrupted. Sit or lie down in a comfortable position, and take a few deep breaths to center yourself.
2. Close your eyes and bring your attention to the physical sensations in your body. Notice any areas of tension or discomfort. Breathe into these areas, acknowledging them without trying to change them.
3. Allow yourself to name the emotions you're feeling. It could be anger, sadness, fear, or something else. As you identify each emotion, silently say to yourself, "It's okay to feel this."
4. Give yourself permission to sit with each emotion for a few moments. Don't try to push it away or hold onto it. Just let it be.
5. When you feel ready, take a few more deep breaths and gently bring your focus back to the present moment.

This exercise can help you start to feel more comfortable with the emotions that arise from pain. It teaches you that emotions are not threats; they are simply parts of the human experience. By sitting with them, you begin to strip away their power to overwhelm you.

Moving Forward with Understanding

The initial shock of pain is never easy, but it is a doorway—a chance to step into a deeper understanding of ourselves. As we allow ourselves to feel without judgment, we start to see that pain is not something to be feared or avoided. Instead, it is an invitation to grow, to learn, and to connect more deeply with ourselves. In the chapters to come, we'll explore how to take these first steps further, turning the pain we feel into a source of strength and resilience.

Chapter 3: Choosing to Face Pain

Pain, by its very nature, often leads us to a crossroads. We can try to ignore it, bury it deep, and hope it fades with time, or we can make the brave choice to confront it, to sit with it, and to understand what it has to teach us. This choice is not easy, and it often feels like stepping into the unknown. But choosing to face pain is the beginning of transformation, the first step in turning suffering into strength.

Many people believe that strength lies in suppressing emotions, in "powering through" without looking back. However, real strength comes from vulnerability—the courage to allow ourselves to feel, even when it hurts. Facing pain does not mean wallowing in it or letting it consume us. It means acknowledging it, allowing it to be present without letting it define us. In doing so, we begin to reclaim our power, taking control of our own healing.

The Fear of Vulnerability

Vulnerability is often seen as a weakness, something to be avoided at all costs. Society teaches us to be stoic, to "keep it together" even in our hardest moments. But vulnerability is not a weakness; it is a profound strength. It requires immense courage to allow ourselves to be fully seen, to admit when we're hurting, and to let others into our pain.

Imagine a fortress built to keep out any threat. Inside, it may feel safe and protected, but there is no room for growth or connection. Vulnerability is like lowering the drawbridge and allowing ourselves to step outside the walls. It's a risk, yes, but it's also the only way to truly heal. When we allow ourselves to feel vulnerable, we open the door to understanding, compassion, and connection.

Sample Story

Consider the story of James, a young man who had always prided himself on his independence. After a tough breakup, he felt an overwhelming sadness that he couldn't seem to shake. But instead of allowing himself to grieve, he told himself to "get over it" and move on. He threw himself into work, avoiding any reminder of the relationship or his own pain. Months went by, and while he seemed "fine" on the outside, he was emotionally distant, detached from his friends and family, and increasingly exhausted.

Finally, one night, he broke down. In the quiet of his room, he allowed himself to feel the sadness he had been holding back. He acknowledged the hurt, the loneliness, and even the fear of letting someone in again. As he sat with his pain, he realized that his efforts to avoid vulnerability had only prolonged his suffering. By facing his emotions, he began to understand that the pain was not something to escape but something to learn from.

James's story shows us that while vulnerability can be intimidating, it's also freeing. When we allow ourselves to confront our pain, we take the first step toward healing. We start to see that our suffering is not a burden but a bridge to a deeper understanding of ourselves.

Embracing the Unknown

Choosing to face pain means stepping into the unknown, and this can feel frightening. We may wonder, "What if it's too much to handle? What if I can't cope?" These questions are natural, and they're often signs that we're approaching a place of true growth.

In moments of doubt, it's helpful to remind ourselves that pain, no matter how overwhelming, is temporary. Emotions, like waves, rise and fall. By choosing to face them, we are not inviting endless suffering; we are allowing the storm to pass. Just as we cannot control the tides, we cannot control the intensity of our emotions. But we can learn to navigate them, to trust that we will come through on the other side stronger and more resilient.

The Power of Naming Pain

One of the simplest yet most powerful ways to face pain is to name it. When we name our emotions—whether it's sadness, anger, frustration, or fear—we take away some of their power. Naming helps us understand what we're feeling and why. It gives us clarity and allows us to start seeing pain not as a vague, overwhelming force but as something specific and manageable.

Imagine standing in a dark room. Without any light, every-thing feels ominous, and every sound seems threatening. But when you turn on a flashlight, the shadows start to take shape. You can see what's around you, and the fear of the unknown begins to fade. Naming pain works in a similar way. It brings our emotions into the light, helping us to see them clearly and face them with courage.

Sample Exercise: Naming Your Pain

Here's an exercise to help you practice naming your pain:

1. Find a quiet place where you can be alone with your thoughts. Sit comfortably and take a few deep breaths.
2. Close your eyes and bring to mind the pain you're feeling. It might be something recent or something you've carried for a long time.
3. As you focus on the pain, try to identify the emotions that come up. Ask yourself, "What am I feeling right now?"
4. Write down each emotion you identify. Don't judge or analyze them; just acknowledge them as they are.
5. Once you've listed the emotions, say them out loud if you feel comfortable. This can help you feel more connected to what you're experiencing and more in

control.

Naming your pain doesn't make it disappear, but it does make it easier to face. It allows you to recognize the specific challenges you're dealing with, giving you a clearer path forward.

The Healing Power of Connection

While the journey of facing pain is deeply personal, it doesn't have to be taken alone. Reaching out to others—whether friends, family, or even a therapist—can provide invaluable support. Sharing your pain, even in small ways, can ease the burden and remind you that you're not alone. Sometimes, the simple act of talking to someone who listens without judgment can bring a sense of relief and clarity.

Building connections in times of pain may feel vulnerable, but it is one of the most healing steps we can take. When we share our struggles, we allow others to show up for us, and we give ourselves the chance to feel seen and understood. We also give others permission to share their own pain, creating a community of mutual support and resilience.

Allowing the Journey to Unfold

Healing is not a linear path. There will be days when it feels like progress, and others when the pain resurfaces unexpectedly. This is part of the process, a reminder that growth takes time and that we are allowed to move at our own pace. Choosing to face pain doesn't mean you have to "fix" everything right away. It means that you are committed to staying with yourself, to honoring your journey, and to allowing healing to unfold naturally.

As you continue reading, remember that every small step you take—whether it's naming an emotion, reaching out for support, or simply allowing yourself to feel—is a victory. You are choosing to turn pain into power, to face life's challenges with courage and compassion. This journey is not easy, but it is worth it, and you don't have to walk it alone.

Chapter 4: Learning from Pain

Once we have chosen to face our pain, the journey of transformation truly begins. Pain, as difficult as it may be to endure, is also one of life's greatest teachers. It offers lessons we cannot find in comfort, insights we may miss in ease. While we rarely choose pain, we can choose to learn from it, to look beneath the surface and discover the wisdom it has to offer.

Pain can reveal truths about who we are, what we value, and where we need to grow. It can show us our strengths and our vulnerabilities, our capacity for resilience and our need for compassion. When we approach pain with curiosity and openness, we begin to see it not as an enemy, but as a guide—a force that, while challenging, can lead us toward a deeper understanding of ourselves and the world around us.

Finding the Lessons Within

The first step in learning from pain is to ask ourselves what it is trying to teach us. This does not mean seeking easy answers or trying to justify our suffering. Instead, it's about exploring the ways pain has affected us and what we can take from the experience to shape a more resilient, compassionate self.

Consider the different aspects of your life that pain may touch—relationships, personal boundaries, self-worth, and goals. Pain often highlights areas where we need to grow or change. For example, the end of a relationship may teach us about the importance of setting healthy boundaries or recognizing red flags early on. A career setback might reveal our true passions or push us to develop new skills. Each instance of pain, no matter how small or large, carries the potential for growth.

Sample Story

Sofia's story is a perfect example of this. After a long-term friendship ended abruptly, she felt lost and betrayed. She questioned herself, wondering if she had done something wrong or if she had missed signs along the way. But as Sofia reflected on the relationship, she began to see things differently. She realized that she had often sacrificed her own needs to keep the friendship going, constantly compromising her boundaries to avoid conflict.

Through her pain, Sofia learned the importance of respecting her own needs and setting boundaries. She realized that true friendships are built on mutual respect and that she deserved to be treated with kindness and consideration. This lesson, though hard-won, became a cornerstone of her personal growth. It taught her to value herself more deeply and to seek relationships that nurtured her, rather than drained her.

Sofia's experience shows us that pain, though painful, can also be illuminating. By taking the time to reflect, she transformed her suffering into a powerful lesson that would serve her for the rest of her life.

Seeing Pain as Part of the Human Journey

One of the most challenging aspects of pain is feeling isolated, as though we are the only ones going through it. But pain is universal; it connects us to others and reminds us of our shared humanity. Every person you encounter has faced or will face hardship in some form. Recognizing this can help us feel less alone and more compassionate toward ourselves and others.

When we see pain as a part of the human journey, we stop viewing it as something to be ashamed of or hidden away. Instead, we understand that pain is a thread that runs through every life, binding us together in a tapestry of resilience and growth. Each time we face our own pain with courage, we contribute to this shared story, reminding ourselves and others that we are not alone.

Embracing the Growth Mindset

One of the most powerful tools for learning from pain is adopting a growth mindset. This mindset, popularized by psychologist Carol Dweck, is the belief that our abilities and intelligence can be developed through effort and learning. While it's often applied to academic or career goals, the growth mindset is equally valuable in emotional and personal development.

When we approach pain with a growth mindset, we see it as an opportunity to learn and evolve. Instead of asking, "Why is this happening to me?" we ask, "What can I learn from this?" This shift in perspective allows us to take ownership of our healing and to view each painful experience as a stepping stone toward greater resilience, wisdom, and self-awareness.

Sample Exercise: Reflecting on Pain as a Teacher

If you're ready to start learning from your pain, here's a simple exercise to help you explore the lessons it may hold:

1. Find a quiet place where you feel safe and comfortable. Take a few deep breaths to center yourself.
2. Think of a recent painful experience. It could be something big, like a breakup, or something smaller, like a disagreement with a friend.
3. Ask yourself the following questions, and write down your answers if it helps:
    - What emotions did this experience bring up for me?
    - Did this experience reveal any personal patterns, habits, or beliefs?
    - Is there a lesson here that could help me grow, even in a small way?
    - How can I apply this lesson to future situations?
4. Take a moment to appreciate the insights you've gained, even if they feel small. Remember, growth is often gradual, and each step forward is a victory.

This exercise encourages us to see pain not just as something to endure, but as a source of wisdom. By examining our experiences, we can begin to transform them into valuable lessons that empower us moving forward.

The Role of Self-Compassion

As we reflect on the lessons of pain, it's important to approach ourselves with compassion. Learning from pain is not about judging ourselves or finding fault in our past choices; it's about understanding ourselves more deeply. Self-compassion allows us to hold space for both our strengths and our flaws, to forgive ourselves for past mistakes, and to honor the journey we're on.

When we practice self-compassion, we learn to be gentle with ourselves, especially in moments of struggle. We remind ourselves that growth is a process, not a destination, and that it's okay to stumble along the way. Self-compassion is the foundation of healing, giving us the strength to face our pain with kindness and understanding.

Sample Story

Leah's experience shows us the power of self-compassion. After failing an important exam, she felt devastated. She blamed herself, feeling that she had let herself and her family down. But over time, Leah began to approach her failure with a different perspective. She acknowledged her disappointment, but she also reminded herself of the effort she had put in and the courage it took to try.

Instead of viewing her failure as a reflection of her worth, Leah saw it as an opportunity to grow. She realized that she could learn from her mistakes, refine her study habits, and try again. With self-compassion as her guide, she turned her pain into a source of strength, and she ultimately passed the exam on her second attempt. Leah's story shows us that when we approach pain with kindness and patience, we create the space to learn and grow.

Moving Forward with New Wisdom

As we learn from pain, we begin to see it as more than just a source of suffering. Pain becomes a mirror, reflecting our deepest truths and revealing our inner strengths. It teaches us resilience, empathy, and humility. It reminds us of our capacity to endure and grow, even in the face of hardship.

Moving forward, remember that each painful experience carries its own wisdom. You don't have to find the lesson right away, and sometimes the insights come slowly, over time. But by staying open to what pain has to teach, you allow yourself to grow in ways you may never have thought possible. This journey is not always easy, but it is profoundly transformative, and it leads us to a place of greater understanding, strength, and peace.

Chapter 5: Rebuilding with Purpose

Once we have faced our pain and learned from it, we stand at a new beginning. We are no longer the same people we were before; our experiences have changed us, and we carry within us new wisdom, strength, and understanding. Now, it's time to take what we've learned and use it to rebuild—this time with purpose, clarity, and intention.

Rebuilding after pain is a chance to redefine who we are and what we want from life. It's an opportunity to let go of what no longer serves us, to embrace the things that truly matter, and to build a foundation that is rooted in authenticity and resilience. This process isn't about erasing the past or pretending our pain never happened. Instead, it's about honoring our journey and creating a life that reflects the person we've become.

Discovering What Truly Matters

Pain has a way of stripping away illusions, forcing us to confront our deepest values and priorities. In the aftermath of hardship, we often gain a clearer sense of what really matters—whether it's relationships, self-care, personal growth, or simply peace of mind. This clarity is a gift, a guiding light that can help us shape a life that is meaningful and fulfilling.

Take some time to reflect on what matters most to you. What values do you want to live by? What brings you joy, peace, or a sense of purpose? Pain may have shifted your perspective, revealed new priorities or highlighted things you once took for granted. Embrace this clarity, and use it as a foundation for the life you want to build.

Sample Story

When Mia lost her job, she was devastated. Her career had been her identity, and without it, she felt lost and uncertain. But as she began to process her pain, she realized that her job had never truly fulfilled her. She had always wanted to pursue art, but she had put it aside, thinking it wasn't "practical." Her job loss became an opportunity to reconnect with her passion. She began painting again, eventually turning her art into a small business that brought her a sense of purpose and joy she had never felt before.

Mia's story shows us that rebuilding after pain is a chance to realign with our true passions. It's a chance to let go of the things we pursue out of fear or obligation and to embrace the things that bring us alive. When we rebuild with purpose, we create a life that reflects who we are at our core, a life that feels meaningful and true.

Setting Intentions for the Future

Rebuilding with purpose involves setting clear intentions. Intentions are different from goals; they are not about specific achievements but about how we want to live and who we want to become. Setting intentions gives us a sense of direction, a reminder of the values and qualities we want to cultivate.

Consider setting intentions that reflect the wisdom you've gained from your pain. For example:

- "I intend to prioritize my well-being and make time for rest."
- "I intend to build relationships that are based on trust and mutual respect."
- "I intend to embrace challenges with courage and resilience."
- "I intend to stay true to my values, even when it's difficult."

These intentions act as a compass, guiding you as you move forward. They help you make decisions that align with your values and remind you of the lessons you've learned along the way.

Creating Healthy Boundaries

One of the most powerful ways to rebuild with purpose is to create healthy boundaries. Pain often teaches us about the importance of boundaries—whether it's protecting our time, prioritizing our needs, or maintaining emotional distance from toxic influences. Boundaries are not walls; they are lines that define what is acceptable and what isn't. They are a way of honoring ourselves and creating a space where we can grow and thrive.

As you rebuild, consider the areas of your life where boundaries are needed. Ask yourself:

- Are there relationships that drain my energy or diminish my self-worth?
- Are there habits or commitments that no longer serve me?
- How can I protect my time, energy, and well-being?

Creating boundaries may feel uncomfortable at first, especially if you're used to putting others' needs before your own. But remember, boundaries are an essential part of self-care. They allow you to nurture your own growth and to build a life that respects your needs and values.

Sample Story

After years of putting others first, Julia finally realized the toll it was taking on her health and happiness. She was constantly exhausted, stressed, and struggling to find time for herself. When she experienced a health scare, it was a wake-up call. Julia knew she needed to start setting boundaries, even if it meant disappointing others.

She began by saying no to commitments that didn't align with her priorities. She limited her availability to people who drained her energy, and she started carving out time each day for self-care. Over time, Julia felt a renewed sense of peace and balance. She learned that setting boundaries wasn't selfish—it was a way of honoring herself and creating space for the things that truly mattered.

Julia's journey shows us that boundaries are an essential part of rebuilding with purpose. They allow us to protect our energy, focus on what matters, and build a life that supports our well-being.

Embracing Change and Adaptability

Rebuilding with purpose requires a willingness to embrace change. Pain often changes us in ways we don't fully understand until much later. We may find ourselves drawn to new interests, new people, or new ways of thinking. Embracing these changes allows us to grow and adapt, to move forward without being bound by who we used to be.

As you rebuild, give yourself permission to evolve. You don't have to fit into old molds or live up to past expectations. Let go of what no longer serves you and be open to the possibilities that lie ahead. Trust that each change, even if it feels uncertain, is part of your journey toward a life that feels more authentic and fulfilling.

Sample Exercise: Visualizing Your Ideal Life

If you're ready to start rebuilding, here's a simple exercise to help you visualize the life you want to create:

1. Find a quiet space and sit comfortably. Take a few deep breaths to clear your mind.
2. Close your eyes and imagine your ideal life. Think about the values, relationships, and activities that bring you joy and peace. Picture yourself living in alignment with your true self.
3. Ask yourself the following questions:
   - What kind of relationships do I want to cultivate?
   - How do I want to spend my time and energy?
   - What values do I want to embody in my daily life?

4. Write down any images, words, or feelings that come to mind. Use this vision as a guide as you move forward, making choices that bring you closer to the life you've envisioned.

This exercise helps you clarify what matters to you and gives you a sense of direction as you rebuild. Each decision you make from this place of clarity brings you one step closer to a life that feels meaningful and true.

Moving Forward with Confidence

Rebuilding after pain is not about erasing the past or becoming someone new. It's about taking what you've learned, honoring the journey you've been on, and using it to create a life that reflects your strength, resilience, and wisdom. This process may be gradual, and there will likely be setbacks along the way. But each step forward is a testament to your courage and growth.

As you move forward, remember that you have the power to shape your life. You have the wisdom gained from pain, the strength developed through hardship, and the clarity of purpose that comes from self-reflection. Trust yourself, honor your journey, and know that you are capable of building a life that feels deeply fulfilling and true.

Chapter 6: Harnessing Inner Strength

As we rebuild and reshape our lives after pain, we begin to uncover a strength we may not have realized we possessed. This inner strength is not just about endurance; it's a resilience born from facing hardship, a courage drawn from overcoming obstacles. The journey through pain has shown us what we are capable of, and this strength becomes a powerful ally as we face future challenges.

Inner strength is the quiet confidence that, no matter what we encounter, we have the tools to navigate it. It's the belief that we can handle setbacks, face uncertainty, and continue to grow. This strength doesn't mean we won't feel fear or doubt; rather, it means we have the courage to move forward despite them.

Recognizing Your Resilience

The first step in harnessing inner strength is to recognize the resilience you've already built. Often, we downplay our achievements or overlook the progress we've made. But resilience isn't just about surviving difficult experiences; it's about the growth and transformation that come from them.

Take a moment to reflect on the challenges you've overcome. Consider how each experience has shaped you, what it has taught you, and how it has strengthened you. Recognize that you are stronger, wiser, and more capable because of what you've been through. This acknowledgment is a powerful reminder that, whatever challenges lie ahead, you are equipped to face them.

Sample Story

After a difficult divorce, Liam felt like his life was in pieces. He struggled with self-doubt, wondering if he would ever feel whole again. But as he took steps to rebuild his life, he realized just how resilient he was. Each small victory—finding a new place to live, making new friends, rediscovering his passions—was a testament to his inner strength.

Over time, Liam came to see his resilience as one of his greatest strengths. His divorce had been painful, but it had also shown him that he could adapt, rebuild, and thrive. This realization gave him the confidence to pursue new goals and face challenges with a sense of hope and courage.

Liam's journey reminds us that resilience is not about avoiding hardship; it's about finding the strength to keep going, even when things seem uncertain. By acknowledging our resilience, we honor the journey we've been on and recognize our capacity to face whatever comes next.

Building a Toolbox for Future Challenges

While resilience is a powerful foundation, it's also helpful to build a "toolbox" of strategies for managing future challenges. These tools are resources and practices that support us in moments of stress, doubt, or difficulty. Having a toolbox allows us to approach challenges with a sense of preparedness and self-assurance.

Here are some strategies to consider adding to your personal toolbox:

1. **Mindfulness** – Mindfulness is the practice of being fully present in the moment. It helps us stay grounded, manage stress, and approach challenges with clarity. Whether through meditation, deep breathing, or simply taking a few moments to pause, mindfulness is a valuable tool for staying centered.

2. **Positive Self-Talk** – Our inner dialogue has a powerful impact on how we feel and respond to challenges. Practice speaking to yourself with kindness and encouragement. Remind yourself of your strengths, achievements, and the resilience you've built.

3. **Seeking Support** – Sometimes, our greatest strength is knowing when to ask for help. Lean on friends, family, or support groups when you need encouragement or guidance. Connecting with others reminds us that we're not alone and that we have a network of support.

4. **Adaptability** – Life is full of unexpected changes. By cultivating adaptability, we learn to navigate

uncertainty with greater ease. Embrace flexibility and remind yourself that you have the capacity to adjust, pivot, and find new solutions when faced with challenges.

5. **Self-Care** – Self-care is not a luxury; it's an essential part of resilience. Make time to rest, nourish your body, and engage in activities that bring you joy. Taking care of yourself strengthens your ability to cope with stress and maintain a positive outlook.

By building this toolbox, you create a foundation that supports you in times of hardship. These strategies are reminders of your inner strength, tools that empower you to approach challenges with resilience and confidence.

Sample Exercise: Building Your Resilience Toolkit

To start building your resilience toolkit, take a moment to think about the strategies that help you feel strong and supported. Here's a simple exercise to guide you:

1. **Reflect on Past Challenges** – Think back to a time when you faced a difficult situation. What helped you get through it? Did you rely on friends, practice mindfulness, or engage in creative activities? Write down any strategies that were effective.
2. **Identify New Tools** – Consider other strategies that you may want to try, such as journaling, setting boundaries, or practicing gratitude. Write down a few tools that you think might be helpful in future situations.
3. **Create a List** – Combine these strategies into a list. This is your resilience toolkit, a collection of resources you can turn to whenever you need support.
4. **Practice Regularly** – Make a habit of using these tools, even in small ways, during your daily life. Practicing resilience-building strategies when things are calm can help you feel more prepared when challenges arise.

This exercise helps you create a personalized set of tools that supports your resilience and reminds you of your inner strength. By cultivating these practices, you reinforce your ability to face adversity with confidence.

Embracing Imperfection and Growth

Harnessing inner strength also involves embracing imperfection. Sometimes, the pressure to "have it all together" can be overwhelming. But true strength doesn't come from perfection; it comes from our willingness to keep going, even when we stumble.

Allow yourself to be human. Accept that you will make mistakes, face setbacks, and encounter moments of doubt. These experiences are not failures—they are opportunities for growth. When we approach challenges with a growth mindset, we see them as chances to learn, adapt, and strengthen our resilience.

Each time you face a challenge with compassion and courage, you reinforce your inner strength. Embrace the journey of growth, knowing that each step, no matter how small, is a victory.

Sample Story

Jordan's story illustrates the power of embracing imperfection. After struggling with anxiety for years, he decided to start a business. At first, he felt overwhelmed by self-doubt, worried that he wasn't "good enough" to succeed. But rather than letting his fear hold him back, Jordan embraced the idea of growth. He reminded himself that mistakes were part of the process and that each challenge was an opportunity to learn.

With this mindset, Jordan approached his business with resilience. He made mistakes along the way, but he learned from each one, building a stronger foundation for his success. His journey taught him that inner strength is not about having all the answers—it's about having the courage to keep trying, even when things don't go as planned.

Jordan's experience shows us that resilience is not about avoiding mistakes; it's about finding the strength to keep going. By embracing imperfection, we free ourselves from the pressure of perfectionism and open ourselves to growth.

Moving Forward with Trust in Yourself

Harnessing inner strength ultimately comes down to trusting yourself. Trusting that you have the resilience to face challenges, the courage to keep going, and the wisdom to make choices that honor your journey. This trust is not about knowing all the answers; it's about believing in your ability to navigate the unknown.

As you move forward, carry this trust with you. Remember the strength you've gained from past challenges, the lessons you've learned, and the resilience you've built. Know that, whatever comes your way, you have the inner resources to face it. You are not defined by your hardships but by the strength, courage, and wisdom you've developed through them.

Chapter 7: Finding Purpose in Pain

One of the most powerful ways we can turn pain into strength is by finding purpose within it. Purpose doesn't mean that we are grateful for the hardships we've faced, nor does it erase the pain we've felt. Instead, it allows us to take something meaningful from our experiences—a sense of direction, a new understanding, or a desire to make a difference.

When we find purpose in our struggles, we transform pain into a source of motivation. We start to see that our experiences, however difficult, have something to offer. They shape who we are, inform how we relate to others, and guide us toward the impact we want to have in the world. Purpose allows us to move forward with a sense of meaning, knowing that our journey has value not just for ourselves, but often for others as well.

Defining Purpose on Your Terms

Finding purpose is a deeply personal process. For some, purpose might mean helping others who are going through similar struggles. For others, it may mean creating something new, advocating for change, or simply living in a way that reflects newfound values. There is no "right" way to find purpose; it's about what resonates with you.

To begin defining purpose on your terms, ask yourself:

- What values have become more important to me

through my experiences?

- What do I want to contribute to the world or to those around me?
- How can I use my experiences to bring positivity or understanding into my life or the lives of others?

Purpose doesn't have to be a grand mission. Sometimes, it's as simple as being kinder to others, prioritizing connection, or creating beauty in the world. Let your purpose reflect who you are and what feels meaningful to you.

Sample Story

After losing her brother, Sarah felt an overwhelming sense of loss and grief. For a long time, she didn't know how to move forward. But over time, she realized that she wanted to honor his memory by helping others who were dealing with similar pain. She began volunteering at a local support group for people who had lost loved ones, offering a listening ear and a compassionate heart.

Through her work, Sarah found a sense of purpose. Her pain became a source of empathy, allowing her to connect with others and help them feel seen and understood. Her journey taught her that purpose doesn't erase pain; it gives it a place in our lives, allowing us to move forward in a way that feels meaningful and true.

Sarah's story shows us that purpose can emerge from even the darkest moments. By using her pain as a source of connection, she found a way to honor her brother's memory and bring comfort to others. Her journey reminds us that purpose often grows from our deepest experiences, guiding us toward a life that feels aligned and intentional.

The Healing Power of Purpose

Purpose has a unique power to heal. When we find meaning in our experiences, we create a narrative that connects our past to our future. This sense of continuity helps us process our pain, giving us a reason to move forward. Purpose shifts our focus from what we've lost to what we can create, from what hurts us to what drives us.

Studies show that having a sense of purpose can improve mental and physical well-being, reduce stress, and increase resilience. Purpose doesn't erase hardship, but it gives us something to hold onto, a reminder that our journey has value. This sense of direction brings comfort and strength, helping us face each day with renewed motivation.

Sample Exercise: Writing Your Purpose Statement

To clarify your purpose, try writing a purpose statement. This doesn't have to be perfect or set in stone; it's simply a way to put your intentions into words. Here's a guide to help you get started:

1. **Reflect on Your Values** – Think about the values that have become more important to you through your experiences. What do you want to prioritize in your life? What brings you a sense of fulfillment or peace?

2. **Identify Your Strengths** – Consider the strengths you've developed through pain, such as empathy, resilience, or determination. How can you use these strengths to contribute to something meaningful?

3. **Write a Purpose Statement** – Combine your values and strengths into a statement that captures your purpose. For example, "I want to use my experiences to support others going through similar challenges," or "I intend to bring kindness and compassion into my daily interactions."

4. **Revisit and Adjust** – Your purpose may evolve over time, and that's okay. Allow yourself to revisit and adjust your purpose statement as your journey unfolds.

This exercise helps you put your purpose into words, giving you a sense of direction and clarity. Your purpose statement can serve as a reminder of your values and intentions, guiding you as you move forward.

Connecting Purpose to Daily Life

Finding purpose is not just about having a guiding principle; it's about incorporating that purpose into your daily life. This might mean taking small steps each day to live in alignment with your values, whether through acts of kindness, creative pursuits, or moments of self-care. Purpose is not a destination; it's a way of being, a choice to live in a way that feels true to who you are.

Here are a few ways to connect purpose to your daily life:

- **Reflect on Your Purpose Each Morning** – Start your day by reflecting on your purpose. Ask yourself how you can bring it into your actions, interactions, or mindset.
- **Engage in Meaningful Activities** – Choose activities that align with your purpose, whether it's volunteering, spending time with loved ones, or pursuing creative projects.
- **Practice Gratitude** – Gratitude helps us focus on the positive aspects of our journey. Take a moment each day to appreciate the growth and insight you've gained from your experiences.

These practices allow you to live your purpose in small, meaningful ways. By integrating purpose into your daily life, you create a sense of fulfillment and direction that carries you through each day.

Sample Story

When Maya was diagnosed with a chronic illness, she felt as though her life had come to a standstill. But over time, she discovered a new sense of purpose: raising awareness and educating others about her condition. She started a blog to share her story, offering information, encouragement, and support to others facing similar challenges.

Through her work, Maya found a way to turn her pain into something positive. Her purpose became a source of motivation, giving her a reason to keep going and a sense of connection to a larger community. Her journey reminds us that purpose can emerge from even the most difficult circumstances, transforming our experiences into something meaningful.

Maya's story shows us that purpose can be a source of healing and strength. By sharing her journey, she not only found fulfillment but also created a space for others to feel seen and supported. Her experience teaches us that purpose is not just about personal fulfillment; it's about creating connections and contributing to the well-being of others.

Finding Purpose in Every Season

Purpose is not a fixed destination. It can evolve as we grow and change, shifting with our experiences and insights. Sometimes, purpose may feel clear and focused; at other times, it may feel uncertain or elusive. Allow yourself to embrace the ebb and flow of purpose, trusting that each season of your life has something meaningful to offer.

Remember, purpose doesn't have to be grand or life-changing. It can be as simple as choosing to approach each day with compassion, making a difference in small ways, or living in a way that feels true to you. Trust that your journey has value, and know that each step brings you closer to a life filled with meaning and fulfillment.

Moving Forward with a Sense of Meaning

Finding purpose in pain is a journey, one that unfolds with each new experience, insight, and choice. This journey doesn't erase the challenges you've faced, but it gives them a place in your life, allowing you to move forward with a sense of meaning. Purpose transforms pain into a source of strength, guiding you toward a life that feels aligned and true.

As you continue on this path, remember that purpose is not about perfection; it's about intention. It's about choosing to live in a way that reflects who you are and what you've learned. Trust in your journey, honor your experiences, and know that you are capable of creating a life filled with meaning, resilience, and fulfillment.

Chapter 8: Cultivating Self-Compassion

As we work through pain and move toward healing, one of the most essential yet challenging practices we can cultivate is self-compassion. Self-compassion is about treating ourselves with the same kindness, patience, and understanding that we would offer to someone we love. It's about recognizing that we are human, that we will make mistakes, and that healing is a journey filled with ups and downs.

When we practice self-compassion, we give ourselves permission to feel, to rest, and to take things one step at a time. Rather than pushing ourselves to "get over" our pain or "move on" too quickly, self-compassion allows us to honor our journey and meet ourselves exactly where we are. It helps us view ourselves with empathy, embracing the parts of us that are wounded and working toward healing.

Why Self-Compassion Matters

In moments of pain, it's easy to become our harshest critic. We may feel like we should be "stronger," or that we're "not handling things well enough." These thoughts can make our healing journey even harder, creating unnecessary pressure and feelings of inadequacy. Self-compassion, on the other hand, softens this inner dialogue, helping us approach ourselves with patience and understanding.

Studies show that self-compassion can lead to greater emotional resilience, lower levels of stress and anxiety, and an improved ability to cope with life's challenges. When we treat ourselves with kindness, we create an environment that fosters healing, allowing us to move forward with a sense of acceptance and peace.

Sample Story

After being laid off from a job she loved, Amelia felt overwhelmed by self-doubt and frustration. She blamed herself, wondering if she could have done something differently. She pushed herself to "get over it" and move on, but the pain lingered, and her harsh inner dialogue only made her feel worse.

Eventually, Amelia began practicing self-compassion. She started journaling, writing down words of kindness to herself, and reminding herself that her worth was not tied to her job. Through self-compassion, she allowed herself to grieve the loss and acknowledge her feelings without judgment. This shift in mindset helped her find peace and renewed confidence, reminding her that healing is a journey that deserves patience and understanding.

Amelia's story shows us the power of self-compassion. By treating herself with kindness, she was able to release the self-criticism that had been holding her back. Her journey reminds us that self-compassion is a gentle force that nurtures healing, allowing us to move forward with acceptance and resilience.

Practicing Self-Compassion in Daily Life

Self-compassion is a skill that we can cultivate through daily practices. These practices may feel unfamiliar at first, especially if we're used to being critical of ourselves. But with time, self-compassion becomes a natural part of our inner dialogue, offering support and kindness whenever we need it.

Here are a few ways to practice self-compassion:

1. **Practice Self-Forgiveness** – Release the need to be perfect or have all the answers. Allow yourself to make mistakes, knowing that they are part of the learning process. Forgive yourself for moments of doubt, fear, or regret, and remind yourself that you are doing the best you can.

2. **Treat Yourself Like a Friend** – When you're feeling down or struggling, ask yourself what you would say to a friend in the same situation. Speak to yourself with the same kindness and understanding, offering words of encouragement and comfort.

3. **Acknowledge Your Feelings Without Judgment** – Allow yourself to feel whatever emotions come up, without judging or dismissing them. Whether it's sadness, anger, or fear, recognize that these feelings are valid and deserve to be honored.

4. **Practice Mindful Self-Compassion** – Mindfulness allows us to be present with our experiences without judgment. When practicing mindful self-compassion, bring awareness to your thoughts and feelings, and

respond with kindness. This practice helps you stay grounded, nurturing self-compassion even in challenging moments.

Sample Exercise: Writing a Letter to Yourself

One powerful way to practice self-compassion is by writing a compassionate letter to yourself. This exercise encourages you to approach yourself with kindness, empathy, and understanding.

Here's a simple guide to help you write your letter:

1. **Choose a Situation** – Think of a situation where you have been hard on yourself, perhaps a recent challenge or moment of self-doubt.
2. **Write from a Place of Compassion** – Imagine you are writing to a friend who is going through the same experience. Offer words of comfort, understanding, and encouragement. Remind yourself that it's okay to feel what you're feeling and that you deserve kindness.
3. **Acknowledge Your Strengths** – Recognize the strengths and qualities that have helped you navigate this experience. Celebrate your resilience, courage, or any other qualities that you bring to the situation.
4. **Revisit the Letter** – When you're feeling down or struggling, revisit this letter as a reminder of your worth and the kindness you deserve.

This exercise helps you cultivate a compassionate mindset, offering yourself understanding and encouragement. By treating yourself with empathy, you create a foundation of self-compassion that supports you in moments of difficulty.

Embracing Imperfection with Self-Compassion

One of the most powerful aspects of self-compassion is that it allows us to embrace our imperfections. So often, we feel pressure to "have it all together" or to handle our pain flawlessly. But self-compassion reminds us that it's okay to be human, to have moments of vulnerability, and to make mistakes.

Embracing imperfection doesn't mean we give up on growth; it means we approach growth with kindness. It means we allow ourselves to stumble, knowing that each step, even the missteps, is part of our journey. By embracing imperfection, we give ourselves the space to heal, grow, and evolve in our own time.

Sample Story

When Carlos lost his mother, he felt a deep sense of grief and sadness. He told himself that he needed to be "strong" for his family, trying to suppress his emotions and push through the pain. But this approach only left him feeling disconnected and overwhelmed.

Eventually, Carlos began practicing self-compassion, allowing himself to grieve without judgment. He reminded himself that it was okay to feel sad, that his grief was a natural part of healing. By embracing his emotions and treating himself with kindness, Carlos found a sense of peace and connection. His journey taught him that strength is not about suppressing pain but about allowing ourselves to feel and heal.

Carlos's story shows us that self-compassion helps us embrace our imperfections and honor our journey. By allowing himself to feel, he created space for healing and connection, discovering that self-compassion is an essential part of resilience.

The Power of Self-Compassion in Moving Forward

Self-compassion doesn't erase pain, but it transforms how we experience it. It softens the harsh edges, helping us navigate difficult moments with grace and understanding. When we treat ourselves with compassion, we create an inner environment that supports healing, allowing us to move forward with resilience and peace.

As you continue on your journey, carry self-compassion with you. Let it be a reminder that you are worthy of kindness, that you deserve patience, and that you have the strength to heal at your own pace. Self-compassion is not about perfection; it's about honoring yourself and embracing each step with a gentle heart.

Moving Forward with Compassion and Courage

Cultivating self-compassion is an ongoing practice, one that requires patience and commitment. But with time, self-compassion becomes a natural part of our journey, offering us comfort and strength whenever we need it. By treating ourselves with kindness, we build a foundation of resilience, allowing us to face each day with courage and grace.

As you move forward, remember that self-compassion is a gift you can give to yourself each day. It's a reminder that you are human, that you are worthy of kindness, and that you have the power to create a life filled with understanding and love. Embrace your journey, honor your experiences, and know that self-compassion will guide you every step of the way.

Chapter 9: Building a Supportive Environment

Healing is not a solitary journey. While our inner work is essential, the people and environments we surround ourselves with also play a critical role in our growth. When we create a supportive environment, we build a foundation that nurtures resilience, encourages us to keep going, and reminds us that we are not alone.

A supportive environment includes the people who lift us up, the spaces that bring us peace, and the boundaries that protect our well-being. By intentionally cultivating this kind of environment, we create a safe space for ourselves—a space that supports healing, self-discovery, and growth.

Recognizing Positive and Negative Influences

The people in our lives have a powerful impact on our journey. Some people inspire us, offering encouragement, empathy, and understanding. Others, however, may drain our energy or trigger negative emotions, whether intentionally or unintentionally. Part of creating a supportive environment is recognizing who and what contributes positively to our life and who does not.

Take a moment to think about the people in your life. Who brings you peace, encouragement, or comfort? Who makes you feel valued and understood? These are the people who form your support system, the ones who uplift you in times of need.

On the other hand, consider those who may drain your energy, dismiss your feelings, or create unnecessary conflict. It's natural to have relationships with people who have different perspectives or personalities, but if someone consistently causes you stress or discomfort, it may be time to reassess that relationship. Setting boundaries with these individuals can help protect your emotional well-being and create space for more positive influences.

Sample Story

After going through a painful breakup, James found himself feeling isolated and overwhelmed. His friends, while supportive, didn't always understand the depth of his pain. But his sister, who had been through a similar experience, offered him unwavering empathy and encouragement. She became his confidante, reminding him that healing would take time and that he was not alone.

With his sister's support, James was able to navigate his journey more easily. He learned the value of having people in his life who understood his experiences and offered encouragement without judgment. His story reminds us that our support system is a crucial part of healing, providing comfort and understanding during even the most difficult moments.

Creating Boundaries that Protect Your Well-Being

Boundaries are an essential part of a supportive environment. They protect our energy, safeguard our mental health, and allow us to prioritize our needs. Setting boundaries is not about cutting people off; it's about creating space to heal and grow in a way that feels safe and empowering.

Here are a few ways to set and maintain healthy boundaries:

1. **Define Your Limits** – Take time to consider what you are comfortable with and what you need to feel safe. This might mean setting limits on how much time you spend with certain people or establishing guidelines for how you want to be treated.

2. **Communicate Clearly** – When setting boundaries, communicate openly and honestly. Let others know what you need in a respectful way. For example, if you need time alone to recharge, express this need without guilt or apology.

3. **Honor Your Boundaries Consistently** – Boundaries are only effective if we honor them. Practice maintaining your boundaries even if others push back, knowing that you are prioritizing your well-being.

4. **Reassess as Needed** – Boundaries may change over time, and that's okay. Revisit and adjust your boundaries as your needs evolve, ensuring they continue to protect your well-being.

Sample Exercise: Defining Your Support System

To build a supportive environment, it's helpful to clarify who and what supports you. This exercise will help you identify the people, spaces, and activities that contribute positively to your life.

1. **List Your Supportive People** – Write down the names of people who offer you encouragement, understanding, and kindness. These could be family members, friends, mentors, or even coworkers.
2. **Identify Positive Spaces and Activities** – Think about the places and activities that bring you peace or joy. This might include spending time in nature, practicing a hobby, or visiting a favorite spot.
3. **Reflect on Negative Influences** – Consider if there are people or environments that drain your energy or negatively affect your well-being. Note these down, recognizing that it's okay to distance yourself from anything that doesn't support your growth.
4. **Set Intentions** – Based on your reflections, set an intention to prioritize positive influences and minimize negative ones. This intention will guide you in creating a supportive environment that nurtures your healing journey.

This exercise offers clarity on who and what supports your growth. By identifying positive influences and setting intentions, you create a foundation for resilience, allowing you to move forward in a way that feels empowered and supported.

Cultivating Self-Support

While our environment plays a significant role in our well-being, it's also important to cultivate self-support. This means becoming our own source of encouragement, setting boundaries within ourselves, and treating ourselves with kindness. Self-support allows us to feel grounded and resilient, even when external circumstances are challenging.

Here are some ways to cultivate self-support:

- **Practice Positive Self-Talk** – Become aware of your inner dialogue, replacing self-criticism with words of kindness and encouragement. Remind yourself that you are worthy of support, both from yourself and from others.
- **Create a Routine of Self-Care** – Self-care is a powerful form of self-support. Develop a routine that prioritizes your physical, mental, and emotional well-being, creating space for rest and rejuvenation.
- **Engage in Activities that Foster Resilience** – Choose activities that make you feel strong and connected, such as exercise, meditation, or creative pursuits. These activities remind you of your inner strength, allowing you to approach challenges with resilience.

Self-support is about being there for ourselves, offering encouragement and care even in difficult times. By cultivating self-support, we build an inner foundation that sustains us, helping us move forward with strength and grace.

Sample Story

When Maria began her journey of healing from trauma, she struggled with self-doubt and fear. But she realized that her environment played a major role in how she felt. She decided to focus on creating a supportive space, filling her home with things that brought her peace—plants, soft lighting, and comforting books. She also began setting boundaries with people who didn't respect her healing journey.

Through these changes, Maria found a sense of calm and resilience. Her supportive environment allowed her to feel grounded, giving her the strength to face each day with courage. Her story shows us that when we create a nurturing space for ourselves, we foster resilience and growth, allowing healing to unfold naturally.

The Importance of Letting Go of Toxic Connections

As we build a supportive environment, it's essential to recognize when certain connections are no longer healthy. Toxic relationships can create stress, hinder our growth, and drain our energy. While it may be difficult, letting go of these connections is sometimes necessary to protect our well-being.

Letting go doesn't mean we harbor resentment or bitterness; it means we prioritize our healing and create space for relationships that honor our journey. It's an act of self-care and self-respect, a way of saying that we deserve to be surrounded by people who uplift us.

Moving Forward with a Supportive Environment

Creating a supportive environment is a gift we give to ourselves. It's a reminder that our journey deserves respect, that our well-being matters, and that we have the power to shape our surroundings in a way that nurtures growth. By surrounding ourselves with positive influences, setting boundaries, and cultivating self-support, we create a foundation of resilience, one that sustains us through every season of life.

As you continue your journey, remember that you deserve to feel supported, safe, and valued. Embrace the relationships, spaces, and practices that bring you peace and strength, and know that each step you take is a testament to your resilience. Your environment is a reflection of your commitment to healing, a foundation that empowers you to move forward with courage, grace, and purpose.

Chapter 10: Embracing Change as a Path to Transformation

Change is one of the few certainties in life, yet it often brings with it feelings of fear, resistance, or uncertainty. When we're faced with change—whether expected or unexpected—it can feel unsettling, challenging our comfort zones and forcing us to confront the unknown. But embracing change can also be one of the most transformative aspects of our journey, opening doors to growth, healing, and new possibilities.

In the process of turning pain into power, change becomes our ally. Rather than something to be feared, change can be embraced as a powerful force that helps us shed old patterns, discover our inner strength, and align with our true path. This chapter explores how we can learn to embrace change, see it as an opportunity for growth, and allow it to lead us toward a more authentic life.

Why We Resist Change

Resistance to change is a natural human reaction. When life feels familiar, we experience a sense of safety and control. Change disrupts that sense of control, bringing uncertainty and challenging us to adapt to new circumstances. It's normal to feel resistant, even fearful, of what lies ahead.

However, resistance often keeps us stuck, preventing us from moving forward. When we resist change, we limit our ability to grow and evolve. By understanding why we resist change, we can begin to release that resistance, opening ourselves up to the possibility that change, while uncomfortable, may bring growth and transformation.

Sample Story

After working in the same job for over a decade, Sarah was devastated when her company downsized, and she lost her position. She felt lost, unsure of what to do next. The change felt overwhelming, and she initially resisted the idea of moving forward, clinging to the comfort of her past job.

But with time, Sarah began to see the change as an opportunity. She explored new career paths, took classes to develop her skills, and eventually found a job that she felt passionate about. Looking back, she realized that losing her job was a pivotal moment that allowed her to pursue a career that aligned more closely with her values and interests. Sarah's story reminds us that while change can be painful, it can also open doors to unexpected and fulfilling paths.

Embracing Change as an Opportunity for Growth

When we embrace change, we allow ourselves to see it as a stepping stone toward growth. Change can push us to expand our horizons, develop new skills, and deepen our self-awareness. It challenges us to adapt, to rethink our beliefs, and to discover parts of ourselves that we may not have known existed.

Here are some ways to embrace change as an opportunity for growth:

1. **Shift Your Perspective** – Rather than viewing change as a disruption, try to see it as a chance to explore something new. Ask yourself, "What can I learn from this? How might this change help me grow?"
2. **Focus on Adaptability** – Change often requires us to be flexible. Embrace adaptability as a strength, knowing that your ability to adjust will help you navigate whatever comes next.
3. **Stay Open to Possibilities** – Change can bring unexpected opportunities. Keep an open mind, allowing yourself to explore new interests, meet new people, and try new experiences. You may discover a path that brings you joy and fulfillment.
4. **Trust the Process** – Change is rarely a smooth journey, but trust that each step is leading you toward something meaningful. Have faith in your ability to handle whatever comes your way, knowing that growth is often a gradual process.

Sample Exercise: Reframing Change

To help you embrace change, try this reframing exercise. It will guide you in shifting your perspective, allowing you to view change as a positive force.

1. **Identify a Change in Your Life** – Think of a recent or upcoming change. This could be a change in your personal life, work, or relationships.
2. **Write Down Your Initial Thoughts** – Write down any feelings of resistance, fear, or uncertainty you have about this change. Acknowledge these feelings without judgment.
3. **Reframe the Change** – Now, consider how this change could lead to growth. Ask yourself, "What opportunities does this change bring? How might this change allow me to learn or evolve?"
4. **Set an Intention for Embracing Change** – Write a positive intention that reflects your commitment to embracing change. For example, "I am open to the growth that this change will bring," or "I trust that this change is leading me toward my true path."

This exercise helps you view change as a positive force, allowing you to release resistance and embrace the possibilities that lie ahead.

Sample Story

When Michael's relationship ended, he felt heartbroken and uncertain about his future. For a long time, he resisted the change, wishing things could go back to how they were. But eventually, he realized that the end of his relationship was an opportunity to focus on himself, to explore his passions, and to create a life that felt fulfilling on his own terms.

Through this change, Michael discovered new interests, made new friends, and developed a deeper understanding of who he was. He realized that while the change was painful, it was also a catalyst for personal growth, one that led him to a more fulfilling and authentic life.

Michael's story illustrates that even painful changes can be transformative, helping us discover strength and resilience within ourselves.

The Role of Letting Go in Embracing Change

A significant part of embracing change is learning to let go. When we hold on tightly to the past, we prevent ourselves from moving forward. Letting go doesn't mean forgetting or dismissing what has happened; it means releasing the attachment to what no longer serves us, making space for something new.

Letting go can be challenging, especially when we're attached to people, places, or routines that once brought us comfort. But when we let go, we free ourselves to experience life in new ways. We allow ourselves to embrace change with an open heart, trusting that the journey ahead will lead us to growth and transformation.

Moving Forward with Courage and Openness

Embracing change is an act of courage. It requires us to step into the unknown, to face our fears, and to trust that we are capable of handling whatever lies ahead. When we approach change with openness, we create the possibility for transformation, allowing ourselves to evolve into the person we are meant to become.

As you continue on your journey, remember that change is not something to be feared; it is a natural part of life, one that can lead to profound growth and self-discovery. Embrace change as a path to transformation, a force that helps you shed old layers and uncover your true potential.

Moving Forward with Resilience and Faith

Life will bring many changes, some expected, others unexpected. But with each change, you have the opportunity to grow, to learn, and to transform. Embrace change with resilience, knowing that you have the strength to navigate whatever comes your way. Trust that each step, each shift, and each new chapter is leading you toward a more authentic and fulfilling life.

Change is a journey—a journey that allows you to rediscover yourself, to heal, and to become the person you are meant to be. Embrace it with an open heart, a courageous spirit, and a deep faith in your ability to grow and thrive.

Chapter 11: Finding Purpose and Meaning in Your Journey

One of the most powerful aspects of our journey is discovering the purpose and meaning behind our experiences. When we go through difficult times, it's natural to wonder, "Why me?" or "What is the point of all this?" But as we continue to grow, heal, and reflect, we can begin to see how our experiences shape us, teach us, and guide us toward a deeper understanding of ourselves and our purpose.

Finding purpose doesn't mean that every painful experience has a clear reason or that all our struggles have an easy explanation. Rather, it means recognizing that even our most challenging moments contribute to our growth, building resilience, empathy, and wisdom. It's about understanding that our journey, with all its highs and lows, has a unique significance—one that can inspire, uplift, and empower us to live more meaningfully.

How Purpose Gives Us Strength

Purpose has a way of transforming our pain. When we find purpose in our journey, our struggles no longer feel random or meaningless. Instead, they become part of a larger story, one that gives us direction and strength. Purpose motivates us to keep going, even when things are tough, because we know that there is something greater, we are working toward.

Finding purpose is not about having all the answers. It's about choosing to see our experiences as meaningful, using them to create a life that reflects our values, passions, and desires. With purpose, we feel a sense of fulfillment and drive, knowing that our journey matters.

Sample Story

Emma, who struggled with chronic illness for years, often felt defeated and hopeless. Her illness had disrupted her life in countless ways, making it difficult for her to pursue her dreams. But over time, Emma began sharing her story with others who were also living with similar conditions. She realized that by sharing her experiences, she could help others feel less alone, offering support and understanding.

Through this, Emma found a new sense of purpose. Her journey, while painful, had led her to a place where she could make a difference. Emma's story reminds us that our purpose often emerges from our challenges, giving us the strength to transform our struggles into a source of hope and connection.

Steps to Discovering Your Purpose

Finding purpose is a unique journey for each person, and there's no single formula that applies to everyone. However, there are some steps you can take to explore what purpose means for you and how your experiences contribute to it.

1. **Reflect on Your Values and Passions** – Start by considering what you truly care about. What are your core values? What are you passionate about? Purpose often aligns with the things that matter most to us, giving us a sense of direction and fulfillment.

2. **Identify Lessons from Your Experiences** – Think about the challenges you've faced. What have you learned from them? How have they shaped you? Recognizing the lessons in your journey can help you see how your experiences have contributed to your growth, pointing you toward a deeper sense of meaning.

3. **Explore Ways to Use Your Strengths** – Purpose often involves using our strengths and abilities to make a positive impact. Consider how you can use your unique talents to support others, bring joy, or create something meaningful.

4. **Embrace Curiosity and Exploration** – Purpose isn't something that arrives all at once. Allow yourself to explore, to try new things, and to be curious about different paths. Purpose often reveals itself over time, evolving as you continue on your journey.

Sample Exercise: Finding Your Purpose Through Reflection

This exercise will guide you in exploring the purpose and meaning behind your experiences, helping you connect with a deeper sense of fulfillment.

1. **Reflect on a Significant Challenge** – Think about a challenge or difficult period in your life. Write down what you experienced, how it affected you, and any emotions associated with it.

2. **Identify What You Learned** – Consider the lessons this experience taught you. Write down any insights or growth that came from it, recognizing how it contributed to your personal development.

3. **Consider How It Can Help Others** – Think about how your experience could be of value to others. How might sharing your story, offering support, or using your skills in a certain way make a positive difference?

4. **Set an Intention for Your Purpose** – Based on your reflections, set a simple intention that captures your purpose. For example, "I intend to use my experiences to uplift others," or "I will embrace my journey as a source of inspiration for myself and others."

This exercise encourages you to see your experiences as part of a larger journey, helping you find purpose and meaning in your path.

Sample Story

After losing his father to cancer, Liam felt a deep sense of loss. The experience was painful, leaving him feeling empty and questioning everything he thought he knew. But as time passed, he realized that his father's strength and resilience had left a profound impact on him. Liam decided to honor his father's legacy by volunteering with cancer support organizations, helping others navigate the challenges his family had faced.

Through this work, Liam found a new sense of purpose. His loss had led him to a place where he could support others, bringing comfort and hope to those in need. Liam's story shows us that even in our darkest moments, we can find a way to turn our pain into something meaningful, using our journey to make a positive impact.

Embracing Purpose as a Journey, Not a Destination

Purpose is not a fixed point that we reach once and for all. It is an evolving journey, one that grows and changes as we continue to learn and grow. Some days, our purpose may feel clear and powerful; on other days, it may feel distant or uncertain. This is natural. The key is to keep moving forward, trusting that each step, each experience, and each lesson is part of the path.

Embracing purpose as a journey allows us to remain open to change and growth. We can let go of the need for all the answers, focusing instead on living with intention, kindness, and curiosity. By doing so, we allow our purpose to unfold in its own time, guiding us toward a life that feels meaningful and fulfilling.

Moving Forward with Purpose and Passion

Finding purpose doesn't mean our journey will always be easy, but it gives us a sense of direction and strength. It reminds us that our experiences have meaning, that our struggles are not in vain, and that we have the power to create something beautiful from our journey.

As you move forward, remember that your purpose is unique to you. It may not look like anyone else's, and that's okay. Embrace the path that feels authentic, allowing your experiences to guide you toward a life that reflects who you truly are. With purpose, you can transform pain into power, creating a life that is rich with meaning, resilience, and fulfillment.

Chapter 12: Embracing a Life of Resilience, Empowerment, and Purpose

As we come to the close of this journey, it's important to reflect on the transformation that comes from embracing life with resilience, empowerment, and purpose. Painful experiences, though difficult, offer us opportunities to grow, to strengthen, and to discover what truly matters. They give us the chance to transform, turning our wounds into sources of strength and our challenges into meaningful chapters in our life story.

For those who have faced heartbreak—the loss of a loved one, or the pain of being left by someone they cherished—this journey can feel especially daunting. When someone we love chooses to walk away, it's natural to feel despair, self-doubt, and a lingering sense of emptiness. Yet, even in this darkness, there is a light—a path forward that leads to healing, self-love, and a life filled with purpose.

Finding Resilience in Heartbreak

Heartbreak is one of the most personal and intense forms of pain we can experience. When we are left behind or abandoned, it can feel as if our whole world has been turned upside down. But, as difficult as it is, heartbreak also offers us the chance to reconnect with ourselves, to rediscover our strengths, and to build resilience.

Resilience is not about suppressing pain or pretending that we are unaffected. It's about facing our pain head-on, allowing ourselves to grieve, and giving ourselves the time and compassion needed to heal. It's about choosing to rise each day, even when it feels difficult, trusting that healing is a gradual process and that, in time, we will come to feel whole again.

Sample Story

After her partner left her for someone else, Olivia was devastated. She had poured her heart and soul into the relationship, and now, she was left with a deep sense of betrayal and emptiness. For months, she struggled to find purpose, feeling as though her world had lost its color.

But with time, Olivia began focusing on her own healing. She leaned on friends and family for support, sought guidance through therapy, and allowed herself to rediscover her passions. Eventually, she realized that while her partner's love had faded, her own love for herself was something no one could take away.

Olivia's story reminds us that even in the face of heartbreak, there is hope. We have the power to rebuild, to find strength within ourselves, and to create a life that feels fulfilling, regardless of what others choose. Her journey shows that our worth is not defined by another's love but by the love and respect we hold for ourselves.

Empowerment Through Self-Rediscovery

After heartbreak, it's common to feel as if we've lost a part of ourselves. In many ways, this is true—relationships often shape us, influence our routines, and become a significant part of our identity. But when a relationship ends, we are given a powerful opportunity to reconnect with who we are at our core.

Self-rediscovery is an empowering process. It invites us to explore our passions, to reconnect with old dreams, and to nurture our well-being. It reminds us that our happiness and fulfillment are not tied to any one person; they are within us, waiting to be cultivated.

Here are some ways to empower yourself through self-rediscovery:

1. **Reconnect with Your Passions** – Think back to activities, hobbies, or interests that once brought you joy. Rekindling these passions can help you reconnect with yourself, bringing a sense of fulfillment and happiness into your life.
2. **Nurture Your Well-being** – Self-care is essential during times of healing. Prioritize activities that help you feel grounded and at peace, whether it's exercise, meditation, journaling, or spending time in nature.
3. **Reflect on What You've Learned** – Every relationship teaches us something about ourselves, our values, and our desires. Reflect on the lessons you've gained, using them to guide you toward relationships

and experiences that align with who you truly are.

Finding Purpose Beyond Heartbreak

One of the greatest gifts of healing is the opportunity to find purpose beyond our pain. Heartbreak, though painful, can lead us to a place of compassion, understanding, and even wisdom. It can help us see ourselves more clearly, encouraging us to live a life that is true to our values and aspirations.

Finding purpose doesn't mean that the pain disappears; rather, it means that we use our pain as a catalyst for growth. It allows us to transform our experiences into something meaningful, using them to inspire, support, or uplift others who may be going through similar struggles.

Sample Exercise: Creating a Vision for Your Future

This exercise is designed to help you envision a future filled with resilience, empowerment, and purpose. It will guide you in embracing a life that reflects your true desires and dreams.

1. **Imagine Your Ideal Life** – Set aside a quiet moment to envision your ideal life. Picture a life that feels fulfilling, empowering, and aligned with your values. What does this life look like? How do you spend your days? Who is a part of this life?

2. **Identify Key Areas for Growth** – Reflect on the areas of your life where you want to grow. These may include personal interests, relationships, career goals, or health. Write down the steps you can take to nurture these areas, helping you move toward your ideal vision.

3. **Set an Intention for Moving Forward** – Based on your reflections, set an intention that will guide you as you move forward. For example, "I am committed to creating a life filled with self-love and purpose," or "I choose to focus on my growth and happiness."

This exercise encourages you to take an active role in creating a future that feels meaningful and fulfilling, reminding you that you are in control of your journey.

Sample Story

After a difficult breakup, Marcus felt lost. His relationship had been a central part of his life, and now that it was over, he struggled to find a sense of purpose. But instead of letting his pain define him, Marcus chose to focus on personal growth. He joined a support group, began volunteering, and eventually discovered a passion for mentoring others who were going through similar challenges.

Through this, Marcus found a renewed sense of purpose. His heartbreak had led him to a place of understanding and compassion, allowing him to make a positive impact on others. Marcus's journey shows us that even the most painful experiences can lead us toward a path of purpose and fulfillment, helping us discover meaning in unexpected ways.

Embracing the Light After Darkness

As you move forward on your journey, remember that there is always light after darkness. Heartbreak, loss, and pain are all part of the human experience, but they do not define us. They are chapters in our story, guiding us toward growth, resilience, and ultimately, empowerment.

When we embrace our experiences with an open heart, we allow ourselves to transform, discovering strength and purpose along the way. Even when we feel broken, there is always hope. The light ahead may be dim at times, but it is there, waiting for us to reach it.

Living a Life of Purpose and Resilience

The journey of turning pain into power is not easy, but it is profoundly rewarding. It invites us to live a life that is authentic, resilient, and purposeful. As you continue on this path, remember that each step, each lesson, and each challenge is part of a larger story—one that is uniquely yours.

Embrace your journey with courage, knowing that you have the strength to navigate whatever comes your way. Allow yourself to find purpose in your experiences, using them to create a life that reflects your true self. With resilience, empowerment, and purpose, you can transform your pain into a source of strength, building a life that is filled with hope, meaning, and fulfillment.

About The Author

Ivy CB is an author, writer, and passionate advocate for personal growth and resilience. With a background in Information Technology and a deep understanding of how the mind navigates adversity, Ivy has dedicated her life to helping others harness their inner strength. She believes that every challenge holds the potential for transformation and that true empowerment comes from embracing vulnerability and using it as fuel for growth.

When she's not writing, Ivy enjoys spending time with her family, swimming, and immersing herself in science fiction novels. She is deeply committed to inspiring others to turn their pain into their greatest source of power.

Don't miss out!

Visit the website below and you can sign up to receive emails whenever Ivy CB publishes a new book. There's no charge and no obligation.

https://books2read.com/r/B-A-ZVVQC-RCCIF

BOOKS 2 READ

Connecting independent readers to independent writers.

Also by Ivy CB

Love in the Metaverse
Love in the Metaverse
Love Beyond the Veil

Standalone
Unshackled: Breaking Free from Fear and Embracing Your
True Self
Where Pain Becomes Power